MORAL DECISIONS

Gerard J. Hughes, S.J.

Darton, Longman and Todd
London

First published in Great Britain in 1980
Darton, Longman & Todd Ltd
89 Lillie Road
London SW6 1UD

ISBN 0 232 51470 4

Printed in Great Britain by
Richard Clay (The Chaucer Press) Ltd
Bungay, Suffolk

Practical Theology Series

Editors' Introduction

The Vatican Council ended in 1965. It ratified for the whole Catholic Church a policy of living the Christian life in closer touch with the perspectives of the Bible: love more than law, community more than hierarchy, affirmation of the world more than distrust, the unique worth of the individual more than uniformity.

The Catholic Church has now had fifteen years of experience of these principles: of the hope they bring, the problems and opportunities of implementing them, and above all our need of them as we face the challenge of the future.

Written for the ordinary Catholic, this series describes where we have got to. It recalls that magnificent view of God's relationship with his People in the world of today and what we have so far done about establishing the Kingdom. It tries to see the implications of all this for the decisions we have to make today as individual Catholics who are members of the Church.

Edmund Flood, O.S.B.
John Coventry, S.J.

CONTENTS

INTRODUCTION

Careless thinking costs lives. Maybe not as obviously as careless driving or drug addiction or war, but still, the cost in human terms of bad moral thinking is very great. Of course it is our actions, the things we do and fail to do, which most obviously damage people, which is why we spend so much time looking at our behaviour when we examine our consciences. But our actions very often simply express our attitudes and convictions, and if our actions do damage, it is often because of the attitudes and convictions behind them. People can be destroyed because of the moral beliefs of others, and whole lives blighted by attitudes to and beliefs about morality which are simply mistaken or misplaced.

Examples spring to mind. If some people, however sincerely, hold racist opinions, other people get hurt. Mistaken views in medical ethics, or on marriage, or on social responsibility will lead inevitably to actions as a result of which people will suffer quite unnecessarily. But it is not just wrong moral conclusions which can do damage. Bad arguments, even when the conclusion is all right, can still put people off, and make them reject the conclusion just because they have seen how bad the arguments are. They might not stop to inquire whether the conclusion could have been supported by better arguments instead. For example, both sides of the debate on abortion seem to me to have made it very difficult to assess their conclusions, simply because of the disreputable arguments which they so often bring forward in support of their views. Much the same could be said of the issues surrounding contraception, or the right to strike, or the value of religious education. Again, inconsistent arguments can easily make people confused; and once they are confused, there is the temptation to abandon any effort to think coherently about moral problems, and resort to hunch, prejudice, or impulse instead—and that is no recipe for human happiness. Again, just as a confused concern for tolerance and Christian forgiveness can give the impression that the difference between right and wrong is of little importance, so, too, a misguided authoritarianism in ethics can simply produce rebellion, and bring the true value of authorities into disrepute. Again, if our concern is too narrowly

1

centred on the answers which are given to moral problems rather than with the evidence and arguments used to support those answers, it is very easy to move from there to an unreasoning dogmatism in ethics; this is itself a moral fault which will ultimately corrode the rest of our moral practice.

Careless thinking about morality also makes for frustration. When Christians argue with one another about morality, or when they argue with others who do not share their faith, it somehow seems especially hard to get anywhere with the discussion. Christians themselves are not very clear about how their religion should affect their arguments, or just how the Gospel should guide their lives, and still less clear about what morality should be like for people who do not believe in the Gospel. What exactly is the relationship between Christian belief and Christian morality, and what is a good argument in ethics actually like?

The harmful inadequacy of some traditional Christian moral argument and the unsettling frustrations of contemporary moral debate can be remedied only if we are willing to make a thorough reappraisal of the framework within which such discussions take place. In short, we need clarity about the *methods* of moral thinking. The reader who looks in these pages for a simple recipe for moral living will, I am afraid, be disappointed. I see no reason to suppose that the complex moral problems of our contemporary world can be simply solved, and still less reason to suppose that the solutions can be neatly packaged into a slender booklet. I think the search for this kind of clarity is a temptation. Perhaps, though, clarity of a different kind can be offered. We might be able to be clearer about how to approach moral problems, and how to recognize good lines of solution; and if we got that far, at least we could be more sure of moving in the right direction even if not all our questions have been neatly answered.

So the first part of this book explores three pairs of contrasting positions. Each of them will, I hope, be easily recognizable as a well-known way of tackling the problems of Christian morality. Some of them are traditional, others represent more recent reactions against tradition. I hope that I have presented them all sympathetically and plausibly, yet I shall argue that each of them tends to obscure the real issues. One might almost say that their very plausibility, and the fact that they all contain so much that is true, is what has made it hard for their defenders to see that more needs to be said. I shall try to show where I think progress can be made and dilemmas resolved without abandoning anything which is essential either to Christian belief or to rational moral thinking. I hope, in short, to break up a few long-jams without doing unnecessary damage in the process. Once we have seen what some bad arguments are like, we might hope to be in a position to construct some better ones.

The second part of the book consists in a positive attempt to construct some guidelines for thinking as a Christian about moral issues. What considerations are relevant? What kinds of mistake can we gradually learn to avoid? What can we reasonably expect in the way of moral unanimity at the end of it all? Will we have any moral principles left? I would hope that once this method of approach has been grasped it will at least help us to come with a fresh eye to our more perplexing moral problems. To be sure, to come with a fresh eye is not to become clairvoyant. A map for a pilgrim Church is but a poor substitute for that knowledge which surpasses all our understanding. While we are used to admitting that we see only in a glass darkly how our moral lives lead us to God, perhaps we need to learn also that we see only darkly what being moral actually requires of us here and now. Pilgrims must be content with progress, and with hope instead of vision.

A final disclaimer before we begin. Many of the issues I shall be dealing with involve highly complex questions in theology and philosophy which, in a book of this size and scope, simply cannot be treated in the full and technical manner they undoubtedly require. Some of these I have tried to cope with more at length in my *Authority in Morals*, to which I refer the reader who would pursue them in greater detail.* Here I have presupposed no particular philosophical or theological expertise. I must beg the reader's indulgence for the places in which this has inevitably led to some degree of oversimplification.

***Authority in Morals*: An Essay in Christian Ethics (London, Heythrop College, 1978).

PART ONE

DILEMMAS IN CHRISTIAN MORAL THINKING

1

CHRISTIANITY AS ETHICS

An American politician is credited with saying how pleased he was that the Arabs and the Israelis were beginning to see the futility of violence as a way of solving their problems, and were prepared to take a more Christian attitude towards one another. The remark is, on the face of it, ridiculous. Yet, taken to its logical conclusion, it betrays an attitude to Christianity which would find a ready echo among ordinary Christians. Many ordinary Christians would say that Christianity is basically about loving one another, about forgiveness, about the need to take a constructive attitude towards injustice rather than being sucked into the whirlpool of retributive violence. In a word, Christianity is basically a morality, a set of ethical norms. And, if this is true, it clearly is something in which even Arabs and Israelis could fully share.

The contrasting position could be illustrated by the criticisms of religious leaders when they summon up courage to speak out on the great moral issues of the day. Should a bishop offer an opinion on abortion, or strikes, or immigration, or Northern Ireland, someone somewhere is almost certain to accuse him of unwarranted interference in things which are no concern of his. Let him get back to his pulpit and talk about God, and leave ethics and politics to the rest of us. Whereas on the first view Christianity is almost nothing except a morality, on the second view Christianity is not really about morality at all, but about religious beliefs in a far narrower sense.

So on the one hand it might appear as if Christianity is so concerned with ethics that its doctrinal content almost disappears; and on the other, the pressure is to concentrate on doctrine to such an extent that Christianity will seem almost irrelevant to many of the major problems of mankind. Both sides will then agree that the general solution to this kind of dilemma is to say that Christianity is concerned both with ethics and with belief. But it is important to discover exactly in what way they try to say this, for that general formula can be understood in ways which are still very different. It will be worth our while to examine the two views in more detail, so as to understand the more extreme positions better, and so that we can begin to see the outlines

7

of a more adequate view of the relationship between Christian belief and morality.

Reducing Christianity to Ethics

Why are people tempted to take the apparently surprising line of reducing Christianity to ethics? I suggest that there are two main lines of thought which have led in this direction.

The first springs from the empiricist philosophy common in Britain and America in the 'thirties and 'forties. According to this philosophy, it was meaningless to speak of anything beyond the realm of our sense-experience. As a consequence, to speak of God was meaningless, and there could be no good grounds for believing in him. So the traditional Christian view that the language of theology and the imagery of religion did succeed in conveying a true (even if incomplete) picture of God and his dealings with men appeared to be totally discredited. Some philosophers who were themselves devout Christians accepted this overall philosophical position, and yet wished somehow to defend religion from the charge of meaninglessness. So they were driven to try to reinterpret religious language in some other way. To do this, they turned to morality. Perhaps the true meaning of religious language could be found in its moral import, and perhaps in this way it could be brought down to earth, so to speak. In this way, they hoped both to respect a traditional religious concern with the moral life, and to salvage religion from the attacks of philosophy.

On these lines, to believe in Christ *meant* to commit oneself to a life of self-sacrificing love; to believe in the resurrection *meant* to see one's moral life as having permanent and ultimate importance. On this view, the books of the Bible did not have to be discarded as meaningless, for their meaning could be given in terms of our moral experience. Nor was their explicitly religious imagery useless, for it provided a background, part mythical, part historical, part literary, which had great imaginative appeal and enormous emotional power in reinforcing commitment to the moral life. To be sure, these passages in the Bible could not be regarded as in any sense *true*; but their importance lay not in their truth, but in their power to inspire and integrate our moral lives. In the same kind of way, a contemporary British politician might appeal to the spirit of Dunkirk in advocating a pay-policy; black Americans might appeal to their roots in the vanished civilizations of Africa to convince their people of their dignity; South African politicians to the biblical stories of the conquest of Canaan to bolster the policies of apartheid, or disorientated industrial men to the stable values of our idyllic rural past. If myth or history—

8

and it really does not matter which—can be pressed into service to illuminate the present and offer an imaginative vision of what we must now do, then it is valuable just on that account. In this spirit, some Christian philosophers tried to reinterpret traditional doctrines by relating them to current ethical concerns. The 'cash value' of religious belief was simply and solely a moral value.

This philosophical approach finds a fairly close parallel in the attitudes of many ordinary Christians to the meaning and practice of their religion. Take for example the popular view of what is required to make a Sunday sermon 'meaningful' and 'relevant'. It has to have a moral. It has to be couched in terms of specific moral behaviour—whether of generosity to the poor, or forgiveness for those who have wronged us, or fidelity to one's marriage vows, or respect for God-given life, or whatever. So, preachers who happily expound the values of family life on Christmas Day find themselves totally bereft of ideas on Trinity Sunday, and their flocks, who find Christmas deeply significant, will also find the doctrine of the Trinity 'not really relevant' and comparatively marginal to their Christian faith. Something of the same development can be seen in the teaching of religion in the higher classes of our schools, where the religious syllabus is almost entirely taken over by moral education. The impression is clearly given that what is central to Christianity is ethics, and the very idea of teaching theology to a sixth form would often be considered an eccentricity. A Glasgow schoolteacher once told me of a girl whose entire account of what it meant to be a Catholic was couched in terms of the avoidance of abortion and contraception. Christianity is ultimately reduced to ethics.

Less primitive, but no less reductionist, are those reinterpretations of Christianity simply in terms of human relationships or social and political action, in which the after-life is an embarrassment and the doctrine of the incarnation no more than a way of focusing attention on the moral teaching and example of Jesus. In short, the first line of thought leading to the reduction of Christianity to ethics springs from a loss of confidence at philosophical and at popular levels that religious belief can be given meaning in any other way.

A second line of thought leads in the same direction. Rather late in the day, Christians have felt the need to respond to Marxist criticisms that the Christian Churches not merely have not led, but have often actively impeded, progress towards social justice and basic human rights. In the past hundred and fifty years, the world has come to see the need for social and political reform; and, with the development of science and technology, has come to believe that this reform now at last lies in our power. If only we had the will to bring it about, we really could make human society a society of justice and peace. Christians look with shame on the muted and belated role so often played in this great movement by the Churches. Reacting against their past indifferences, they are led to say that a theology is valid only in so far as it articulates the contemporary struggle for human dignity and freedom. Theology is to be judged by the moral and political stance which it expresses, and if it fails on this score it is not merely irrelevant, but is positively destructive.

The forces leading to the reduction of Christianity to ethics are thus deeply rooted in the philosophy, culture and political experience of our times. On the other hand, those who take this line have very considerable problems to overcome. At least it is not the traditional Christian view that Christian doctrine means no more than a particular moral code. And if Christianity is no more than a morality, very little would apparently be lost by dropping the theological superstructure altogether. Why should we try to preach Christianity to others, when we could much more easily get them to share in our moral concerns? Furthermore, those who seek to reduce Christianity to ethics cannot also claim that it is their religious faith which gives arguments for their moral crusade. On this view, faith *cannot* provide arguments for ethics. All it can do is provide, at most, support of an emotional and imaginative kind for a moral position which has already been adopted. Indeed, the argument really has to go the other way round. What religious beliefs we are to hold will depend on the moral stance we have already decided to adopt.

Morality Reduced to Theology
Precisely in that last sentence is expressed what the defenders of the opposite position would most object to in what has been so far said. On the contrary, they would insist, the truth and ultimate meaning of morality is to be discovered only in the light of revealed Christian doctrine. This view, too, has its popular and its more scientific defenders.

At the popular level, this view is sometimes expressed by saying, 'Were it not for the fact that I am a Christian, I would see nothing wrong in ———'; and it can be discerned in the suggestion that religious education in schools is a good thing because it lays the foundations for sound morals. Many Christians, if asked why it is that some type of conduct is wrong, or why some other is a duty, would naturally be inclined to reply that such is the teaching of Christ, or the teaching of the Church. Along the same lines, they might be inclined to think that a morality without religion will inevitably be at least inadequate, and perhaps even seriously defective. 'Humanist' morality tends to get

10

rather a bad press precisely because it lacks the finer certainty and clarity which only a morality revealed by God can provide. Thus, for example, someone might argue that from a purely human point of view it is difficult to see why divorce and remarriage should be wrong in every case, but that, in the light of the teaching of Christ, one can see the value and point of a more demanding view of marital fidelity.

More sophisticated theological defences of this position are also on offer. It will be argued by many theologians that the true meaning of human life and human destiny are revealed to us only in Christ. It is in Christ alone that God's design for man has been fully revealed. Here alone we can see who we really are, and where it is that we are going, for it is in Christ that we have been created. Ethics without Christianity will inevitably have an inadequate and distorted picture of human nature. Worse still, if we fail to take Christ as our model, we will have no alternative but to take our morality from ourselves. Yet, as Christian faith teaches, we ourselves are fallen, sinful and corrupt. Our minds are so blinded by sin that we are unable to have any confidence in our judgements about right and wrong, and our desires are so warped by the Fall that they offer no true guide to where our happiness is to be found. The moral teaching of Christ stands in judgement on any merely human morality. A theologian who takes this line will consider it blasphemous, in the strict sense of the word, to suggest that human standards should be the judge of theology, as the first position suggests. Rather, it is God who reveals to us his judgement on our human standards.

Other considerations will reinforce this position. If ethics is not to rest on theology, then apparently it would have to rely on moral philosophers instead; or, if not on moral philosophers, on popular opinion? Neither alternative appears very attractive. Moral philosophers almost seem to take a pride in not giving clear and definite answers to moral problems; and as for popular opinion, while there may indeed have been a heightening of moral sensitivity in some areas of ethics, would it not in general appear that along with the recent decline in Christian belief there has in general been a decline in moral standards? In contrast to all this, the teachings of Christian morality offer a much-needed clarity and, indeed, a very welcome element of challenge. What is wanted is not the seductive open-mindedness of humanist moral debate, but a morality built on the rock of the moral authority of Christ.

Unfortunately this position too, like its opposite, is open to very serious objections. As will appear in subsequent chapters, it is very doubtful whether theology can give to ethics the kind of support which this position requires it to give. More immediately, at least some of the arguments used to support a theological morality are double edged.

11

Is it always clear just what kind of moral conclusions explicitly Christian belief would support? For example, might one not argue that precisely because, for the believer, death is *not* the end of the human person, the Christian can afford to treat death more lightly than his non-believing counterpart? So might it not be argued that it is precisely the Christian who should be in favour of a more rather than a less liberal attitude to, say, suicide, or euthanasia or abortion? Again, if too much is made of the corruption of all human desires, is Christian morality not going to appear to be so counter to all our inclinations that it is altogether dehumanizing? Finally, it is hard to see how the defence of a theologically based morality does not lead inevitably to the view that the moral opinions of non-Christians are very seriously defective. To say the least, this is not an easy nor uncontroversial position to defend. It is not shared by Aquinas, or the whole Catholic tradition in moral theology, and, arguably, it is not held by St Paul either.

Preliminary Compromise

The dilemma presented in this chapter is not a particularly acute one, since neither position is really tenable as it stands. Still, to have set the two views out may help us to see what mistakes have to be avoided. Perhaps we can begin to discern the main outlines of what a Christian morality will have to be like.

The first pitfall to be avoided is to present Christianity as if in the last analysis it were no more than a morality backed by whatever imagery seems to be effective in reinforcing it. I believe that it follows from this that preachers and educators must find a way of sharing and explaining their faith in a way which has meaning in it *without* having to resort to ethics in order to do so. Religious belief is more than ethics; it is a vision of the whole world as created in Christ, saved in him and called to share in his glory. The beauty of this vision is not primarily, still less solely, a moral beauty, and to present it as such seems to me to be quite inadequate. In a book on ethics, this point cannot be further developed, though I believe it to be of central importance for religious education.

Secondly, it must not be forgotten that people with no Christian beliefs may still have the grace of God, and their ethical reflections may still be helped by the grace of God. The morality of a humanist cannot, from the point of view of Christian theology, be considered as no more than the gropings of fallen man without grace. Moreover, it is a gratuitous insult to suggest that humanists are necessarily blind to the finer ideals of human living; and if they are not necessarily blind (any more than Christians are necessarily perceptive) there is no necessity for their morality to be Christian.

Thirdly, it is indeed a travesty of Christianity to suggest that it has no concern with ethics, or to suggest that it is only selectively concerned with moral issues—say, only with issues of personal morality, but not with politics, or social justice or racial harmony. The Christian God requires his people to be moral, and the Christian faith is defectively preached if the impression is given that one can be a Christian without being actively interested in the whole range of moral problems. One might add that the Christian community itself will be an inadequate sign of the Kingdom unless it is seen to be concerned with the living out of justice and respect for human rights, both as regards its own members and as regards others. Too often the impression is given that such concern either does not exist, or that it exists only when it does not conflict with the Church's more narrowly institutional interests. Unless the Christian community is seen to exemplify all that is best in human aspirations, it will not be surprising if its preaching falls on deaf ears.

Taking these three points together, it follows that a theology which leads to a morality which an open-minded non-Christian *could* not accept must itself be a defective theology. The same point can be put in a different way. Even fallen man must be able to recognize the revelation of God when it is offered to him; he must be able to distinguish between true and false claims to be God's revelation. One of the ways in which he will do this is by looking at the moral consequences of an alleged revelation; and if those consequences are unacceptable in human terms, then he will have every reason to say that this *cannot* be the revelation of God. Morality for Christians, therefore, must be built on the same foundations as morality for any human being, and in that sense it must be independent of their Christian theology.

On the other hand, there is a very important truth behind the view that theology must surely make a difference to morality. It is not just that God requires us to live according to a morality which we can learn from elsewhere; it is also that our Christian faith colours and gives a meaning to the Christian moral life which the equally moral lives of non-believers cannot have. A rough parallel might be seen in the case of a Christian doing research in astronomy. He must carry on his research into, say, the origins of the universe on exactly the same footing as his colleagues who have no Christian beliefs. His Christian faith will not help his calculations and experiments, and his conclusions must be able to withstand the normal criticisms of other scientists. Yet the Christian astronomer may also see himself as trying to understand the wonders of God's creation, and he might find that his work illu-

13

minates his faith, and vice versa. Similarly, the Christian must argue for his moral views on grounds which are shared by all human beings alike. Yet for him, to live the moral life is part of his hunger for God and his justice; for him, to feed the hungry is not just a fundamental humanitarian duty, but a response to the presence of Christ in the least of his brethren; to suffer for justice is not only an act of the highest human heroism, but a sharing in the passion of his Lord; to be true to his moral convictions is not just being true to his deepest self; it is to share in the hope of Christ's resurrection. Christian morality does not get its answers from Christian theology; but a truly independent Christian faith gives to morality a depth and richness of meaning, for it can see our moral lives as no less than the revelation of God's love among men.

2

CHRISTIAN MORALITY AS LIFE IN CHRIST

We have just seen, so far in general terms, that Christian morality should be developed independently of Christian theology, but should nevertheless be illuminated and inspired by Christian belief. Where does this leave us with regard to the moral teachings of the Bible, and of the New Testament in particular? We shall adopt the same strategy as before, and develop two contrasting answers to this question. This time, the contrast between the two positions will be sharper, and the resulting dilemma will not be as easy to resolve. But if we try to understand each position as sympathetically as possible, we may be able to discover in what direction progress might be looked for.

Christian Morality as the Imitation of Christ
There is a venerable tradition, as old as the New Testament itself, that the Christian life consists in the imitation of Christ in fidelity to his teachings. So St Paul says that the Corinthians should imitate him just as he imitates Christ. But perhaps the most systematic presentation of this position is to be found in the two books written by St Luke. At least part of his purpose in writing both his Gospel and the Acts of the Apostles was to exhibit the early Christian community as re-living the life of Jesus described in his Gospel. Luke deliberately describes the miracles of the apostles in words which remind the reader of the descriptions of the miracles of Jesus himself. The trial of Stephen contains many verbal echoes of the trial of Jesus. Stephen at his death prays for his enemies, and commends his soul to the Father just as Jesus had done. Stephen, too, sees the vision of the Son of man coming on the clouds of heaven, thus reminding the reader of the answer Jesus had given to the court of the high priests and scribes. Perhaps, also, the account of Peter's escape from prison in Acts is meant to remind us of the resurrection of Jesus. Just as the stone was rolled back from the tomb through no human agency, so the gates of

15

Peter's prison simply fell open. Angels were present in both cases, living reminders of the power of God. Peter is met by an astonished girl who runs to tell the brethren, just as Jesus was met by the frightened women in the garden. More generally, Luke presents Jesus as filled with the Spirit, and the Church as filled and guided by that same Spirit.

These are not mere literary devices. Luke is making an important theological point about the relationship between the Christian life and the earthly life and teaching of the Master. In much the same spirit, St Ignatius Loyola in his *Spiritual Exercises* speaks of being poor with Christ poor, suffering with Christ suffering, tormented with Christ tormented, and sharing in the joy Christ felt at his resurrection. The tradition of the imitation of Christ contains, then, two strands. The Christian must take the teachings of Christ as his own; and, more mystically, his life will truly be a re-living of the life of Jesus. 'I live now not I, but Christ lives in me.' It would seem that to take this tradition seriously must surely call in question the whole independent approach to Christian morality with which we concluded the first chapter. If the Christian life is to be a re-living of the life of Jesus, then we cannot know what the Christian life should be like without using him as a model.

The above account, however, glosses over some very considerable difficulties in this whole approach. The ideal of the imitation of Christ is indeed an inspiring one, but on closer examination it is not as clear as it might at first sight appear. Which features of the life of Jesus is the Christian called to imitate? Nobody would suppose that in order to imitate Christ it was necessary for all Christians to learn Aramaic, or to take up carpentry, or to become a wandering preacher. But the difficulty of saying just *why* these examples are absurd can easily be seen if we consider some more controversial cases. Some contemporary Christians would argue very strongly that we should try much harder to imitate the healing ministry of Jesus, and that the rarity of healings through the Spirit in the modern Church is evidence of a comparative lack of fidelity to the Gospel. With this view St Luke would probably agree, though I suspect that St Paul would have more reservations. But should we also imitate Jesus in his total renunciation of violence and the use of power? Should we ordain married men to the priesthood the better to imitate him, or refuse to ordain women because he did not? Plainly, the mere call to the imitation of Christ has not solved all these problems.

Nor can this kind of difficulty be removed by appealing to the moral teaching of Jesus or the New Testament generally. The popular impression that Jesus spent most of his ministry giving moral teachings simply is not borne out by an examination of the Gospels. Most of his time was spent in trying to explain the coming of the Kingdom, and in trying to help his hearers to understand his ministry in terms of their own Jewish traditions. The major controversies of his ministry were not on the whole about moral issues, but about his own status and credentials, and about his attitude to traditional Jewish theology. To be sure, he did insist on very general moral virtues, such as forgiveness, and on general moral duties such as love of one's enemies, and a care even for the outcasts of Jewish society. He repeatedly stressed that a full commitment to his Kingdom would demand a great degree of self-sacrifice. He spoke of the dangers of riches, and of how a preoccupation with this-worldly matters could distract people from the fundamental choice with which he wished to face them. But it is quite clear that he did not try to give systematic moral guidance on all moral issues, nor specific guidance on more than a very few. It would be hard to find a basis for the whole of morality if one had only the teachings of Jesus to use as a basis.

In any case, the New Testament writers themselves do not seem to have thought that all they had to do was to repeat the moral teachings of Jesus. They seem to have felt themselves quite free (at least within limits) to adapt, change and add to the teachings of Jesus to meet the particular needs of the audience for which each of them was writing. Take, for instance, the parable of the unjust steward. Even the traditional name we give this parable probably misrepresents the point Jesus used it to make. It is not clear that the steward was doing anything he was not fully entitled to do, and in any case the point was not about the details of the bills, but about how willing he was to recognize that a turning point had come in his life, and how immediately he leapt to do something about it. It is for this response, so unlike the response of Jesus' hearers to his own preaching, that the steward is commended. But the evangelist has clearly tried to adapt the parable to make a moral point, and has done so by appending another saying about the correct use of money, and still another about being trustworthy in small things as a prelude to being entrusted with great things. There are several other examples of the same kind, where evangelists have adapted teaching on one topic to serve as a basis for something quite different.

A different kind of editorial activity by an evangelist is probably to be found in the reports of Jesus' saying on divorce. Many scholars would take the view that the occurrence of an exception-clause ('in the case of adultery') in one of the places where this saying occurs probably reflects the practice of a particular Christian community where that exception was allowed. Again, whereas Jesus himself kept the law of Moses, and Matthew's Gospel insists on every detail of it being observed, St Paul and other Christian churches plainly did not see themselves as bound in that way. Their own circumstances were different. Furthermore, St Paul is quite happy to give his own solutions to moral problems without references to the teachings of Christ, which he mentions only rarely in this connection; and other writers are willing to take over moral teaching from pagan sources for the good of their congregations.

All in all, then, the New Testament provides evidence of a much greater creativity than could ever be accounted for by the theory that all that was required was that they repeat the teachings of Jesus.

Christian Morality as Fidelity to the Spirit
The alternative approach starts from the difficulties in the notions of imitating Christ and holding to his teachings which we have just outlined, and seeks a solution to them in the doctrine of the guidance of the Holy Spirit.

The Church, it points out, has always continued to do just what we can already see happening in the New Testament. Under the guidance of the Spirit, it has taken the life and teachings of Jesus as a starting-point and inspiration, rather than as a blueprint. The continuity of Christian tradition, it suggests, is to be found not so much in the repetition of teachings or patterns of life from the past, as in ongoing fidelity to the same Spirit which was Jesus' gift to his Church. After all, the New Testament is a set of books which were not in the first instance written for us at all, but for various first-century Christian communities in the Middle East. We should not use it as a court of appeal for settling our problems, which are not the same as theirs. Rather, we should use it to learn how the first Christians thought, and on what they based their conclusions about who Jesus was, about ethics, about their future hopes, and so on. We learn from them a whole Christian attitude to life which we must then translate into our own idiom, for our own day, and in response to our questions. The key notion for the contemporary Christian is not repetition or imitation, but openness to the Spirit. Neither a wooden appeal to the texts of our Christian past, nor recourse to the arguments of secular moralists, can possibly do justice to the demands of the Spirit on us, as individuals and as a community, here in our world now.

The problems with this approach are obvious enough. If the notion of openness to the Spirit is not held in check either by tradition or by independent moral reasoning, then there seems to be no limit on what might not be claimed to be the demands of the Spirit. I recall an instance of a Christian community which was awakened by its leader at 2 am and informed that he had just been required by the Spirit in a dream to visit the sick. The local hospital had to call in the police when all attempts to persuade the visitors that their attentions were inopportune and undesirable had been met with the reply, 'Who are you to question the Spirit of God?' The example is ridiculous, almost tragic. It might seem like an unfair attempt to discredit a position by appealing to an extreme instance. But the logic of the visitors was unassailable. If other positions are more respectable, it is because, tacitly or explicitly, they rely on more than the bare notion of openness to the Spirit. If so, they need to spell out what this 'more' might be.

Vocation in Christ

At first sight, any hope of a compromise between these two positions seems slim. The second rejects in so many words that the New Testament writings can be used to settle matters once and for all, whereas the first would hold that this is just how we should use them. Conversely, what in the second view is regarded as an invitation to a creative response to the call of the Spirit in our time, the first position would see as a dangerously open-ended attitude, all too likely to confuse the call of the Spirit with the whims or fashions of the moment. How, then, are we to proceed?

The case against naïve imitation of Jesus and simple repetition of his sayings is, I think, unanswerable. After all, even Acts does not present the disciples as simple carbon copies of Jesus, and the Church from New Testament times on has never in fact been content simply to repeat what he said. For example, there is just as good evidence that Jesus taught the renunciation of all violence as that he forbade divorce, and just as good evidence that he forbade all oaths as that he forbade lustful thoughts. Yet Christian tradition has by no means treated all these sayings in the same way. Despite the impression that is sometimes given, Christian tradition has never settled its problems *just* by appeal to texts or teachings from the past. This appeal has always been supplemented by something else—moral philosophy, or a theory of authority in the Church or simply an unconscious selectivity about which texts are to be taken as important.

Secondly, it is surely right to say that whatever we have to learn from our forebears or from Jesus himself, it cannot be to respond to our problems in their way, nor to assume without further inquiry that their problems are the same as ours. Imagine a young couple who thought that the way to reproduce in their own lives the happy marriage of their parents was to take exactly the same decisions as their

19

parents did on every point. It is no less absurd to suggest that, for example, all our bishops should have had previous experience in an ordinary job just because most of the apostles did. This might be a good policy, or it might not. It depends on whether, and to what extent, our situation is comparable to that in which Jesus called his first apostles—and we cannot judge that just by seeing what Jesus did. So, to renounce violence, or to forbid divorce, might be as good advice for us as it was for the disciples of Jesus—but it might not. Again, it all depends on whether our situation is morally comparable in all respects to theirs. Mere quotation of the sayings of Jesus will not settle *that* question for us.

Thirdly, it is no good reacting to these difficulties simply by saying that all we have to do is listen to the Spirit. How are we to tell whether it is the Spirit we are listening to, or whether it is simply our own mistaken convictions? And if we try to answer that question by saying, 'Listen to the Church,' the difficulty is merely postponed. For it still remains to be asked how the Church is to decide what to say, and on what principles it will interpret its own tradition. In short, what emerges from this discussion is, once again, the need to have some criteria—some method of using our God-given minds to reflect coherently on our moral problems. Not that we cannot learn from the past—whether from Jesus himself, or from the great Christian saints or even from our own past mistakes. But learning from the past is itself an exercise of moral judgement, not a way of avoiding having to make any moral judgements.

Finally, we can perhaps learn what the true value of the imitation of Christ can be. Once we have learnt to think morally for ourselves, and have discovered some method for doing so well, we can then use this ability to try to understand the teachings and life of Jesus. We can then try to discover what it was about his life and circumstances that would have led him to respond as he did. We will discern in him an unselfishness, a total concern for others, a heroism in his unique vocation, a compassion and a strength which, through the gift of the Spirit, he would share with us. In him we might then begin to see what it is for a man fully to reveal God in a human life, and so to see where we might begin to do so in our lives. Yet we will be aware that his life was but one human life, and that it was a different life from that of each one of us. His actions will not be ours, nor his words necessarily our words. Even so, our vocation to make God's love available to others through our daily lives is a share in his vocation, and the Spirit is in us as it was fully and perfectly in him. Truly we do live in him, with his life; and to the extent that we succeed in coming to grips with our moral problems we know that we will have been helped by his

20

Spirit. It is here that the notion of the imitation of Christ really finds its place; for then we might be able to see in our lives something of a family resemblance to his, and rejoice in the knowledge that we are his brothers and sisters.

3

CHRISTIAN MORALITY AS OBEDIENCE

Recent arguments about Christian morality have been made more difficult by a polarization between those who see morality as obedience to one's conscience and those who see it as obedience to some authority. Indeed, a case can be made by saying that it is this dispute, in the last analysis, which lies beneath all the others, including those we have examined in the previous chapters. The main lines of the disagreement are familiar, and may be briefly set out. Resolving the dilemma will take us to the heart of the central problems in thinking in a Christian manner about moral problems.

Obedience to One's Conscience

Somewhat paradoxically, the view that to be moral consists in following one's conscience can be based on the best authorities. St Thomas Aquinas held that one was bound to follow one's conscience even when it was mistaken. He held this view in both directions, so to speak; it would be sinful to do something one thought to be wrong even if it was in fact the right thing to do; and it would be one's duty to do what one thought to be right even if in fact it was the wrong thing to do. In much the same way, to jump seven centuries, Vatican II speaks of the dignity of man's conscience in this way, 'Conscience is the secret core and sanctuary of a man. There he is alone with God, whose voice echoes in its depths.' The Council goes on to say that this is still true even if a man's conscience is mistaken, provided only that he genuinely cares for truth and goodness and is not blinded by habitual sin. It is a violation of man's greatest dignity as a moral being to force him to act in a manner contrary to his conscientious beliefs.

There are good arguments for this view. We do not in general excuse people's misdeeds just because they were acting under orders, for there are some orders which a person has a duty not to carry out. Before submitting to any authority, we have a duty to consider what that authority asks us to do; and even authorities with apparently impeccable credentials may turn out upon closer acquaintance to be unacceptable in their demands. Since we must make a conscientious judgement about the acceptability of an authority before submitting to it, and of its orders before obeying them, it follows that conscience must be more basic than any authority.

In any case, no authority could possibly make it unnecessary for the individual to have to make any further moral decisions once he has submitted to it. There are two reasons for this. In the first place, there are always going to arise unforeseen situations for which the guidance of authority is not sufficient, and where it is not practicable to seek a further ruling before decisions have to be taken. Secondly, it must be remembered that the subordinate has to be able to *recognize* the situations his superior had in mind in issuing the order. Two rather different examples will illustrate this point. Suppose an employee has been told by his boss not to make too many difficulties in satisfying the demands of the important customers. He still has to be able to tell which the important customers are, and this will be a matter of judgement in every case. It will not help him simply to repeat his orders. Again, when a law has been passed by Parliament, it is the function of a judge to apply it to the cases which come before him. It is not his job to question the wishes of Parliament in the way in which he conducts his court. Suppose, then, that he is trying a case in which someone is accused of incitement to racial hatred. The judge has to be able to decide what conduct would amount to incitement in a particular case, and merely repeating the law to himself will not make *that* judgement for him. Similarly in moral matters. Even if an individual sets himself to obey a moral authority, his own moral judgement will still be required to recognize the situations which the authority had in mind. A girl might set out to obey her mother's request that she should not accept a lift home from a party from anybody her parents do not know. She might still have to decide whether that includes the local vicar and his wife who have come to collect their daughter. A doctor might be quite clear that he should not go to extraordinary lengths to keep a patient alive; but he still has to use his moral and his medical judgement to decide just what would count as 'extraordinary' in the case of a particular patient.

In the end, the most that any authority can do is to give some guidance to the individual conscience. But the bedrock of morality is the conscience itself, which must decide which authorities to obey and when, and whether or not a particular situation is covered by what was authoritatively said.

Obedience to Authority

From an opposite point of view, it will be argued that it would be all very well to speak simply of people following their consciences if only people were always ideally well balanced, well informed, and not liable to have their judgement warped by emotional involvement, or prejudice, or sheer inexperience. But we are all only too well aware of our own shortcomings in each of these respects. We would surely feel insecure—not neurotically, but justifiably insecure—were there no external guidance by which we could make our moral judgements. In moral matters, we need clarity. To leave everything to our own consciences would be to leave ourselves confused, uncertain, and liable to have to shoulder a quite unnecessary burden of guilt.

In this respect, morality is no different from many other areas of our lives, in which the need for authorities is quite clear and acknowledged. Students need textbooks on which they can rely, and people need to consult lawyers and doctors, maps and timetables, dictionaries and *Hansard*. Human life simply could not function comfortably in society, especially not in a society of any complexity, unless there were authorities which could be relied upon. Is there any reason to suppose that our moral lives are any different? It is surely a mark of moral adulthood, not moral infantilism, to be able to recognize when one is simply not competent to decide things for oneself, and to be willing to seek and take proper moral advice.

Furthermore, if all that could be said about morality were that people should follow their consciences, the only result would be that more and more people would be needlessly hurt. In a famous Peanuts cartoon, Charlie Brown walks disconsolately from the baseball field where he has been defeated 47–0 saying, 'I can't understand it, we're so sincere!' But sincerity is no substitute for good coaching. Neither is a stress on personal integrity any substitute for good moral judgement. It is here that the Church comes in. It is part of Christian belief that the Holy Spirit guides the Church in the way of salvation. Does it not follow that the moral guidance of the Church is always preferable to the judgement of the individual, and that it is by following the teaching of the Church that the individual can be sure that his conscience is well informed?

Authority in Morals

The debate between these two positions could not have lasted as long as it has unless there really were a good deal of truth on both sides. Nor could the debate have become as deadlocked and frustrating as

24

it has unless the issues had become rather confused, and the two parties were somewhat at cross-purposes.

Some clarity might be introduced into the argument if we recognize from the outset that each side is in large measure right, but that they are right about different things. To see this, we must remember that it is one thing to be blameless in what one did, and quite another to have done the right thing. All of us can think of cases where we acted as we honestly thought to be for the best at the time, but where what we did turned out to be disastrous. We might still say that, as things seemed then, there was nothing else we could have done; and yet we might regret what we did, and admit that we would never have considered acting as we did if only we had known. Did we do the right thing, then? Our ordinary English usage tends to confuse us here. The phrase 'the right decision' can be used to mean 'the decision which turned out to be the correct one' or 'the decision we could not be blamed for having made'. We cannot be blamed for following our conscience—our honest moral opinion. In that sense, to follow one's conscience is always the right thing to do. But equally we can say that in following our conscience we did something which turned out very badly—and in *that* sense it was the wrong thing to have done. It all depends on which sense of 'right' and 'wrong' one is using.

Perhaps it is a help to see those who urge the primacy of conscience as stressing primarily one sense of what is 'right'. To follow one's conscience honestly and sincerely is always to be blameless; and not to do so is always blameworthy. Those who stress the importance of authority insist that it is important that the decisions we take should be the ones which will turn out well—should be the 'right' ones in the other sense. This is why they so frequently emphasize that conscience should be well informed. Looked at in this way, each side is saying something which is very important and true. They are not, so far at least, contradicting each other at all, but emphasizing two complementary aspects of morality.

A very similar ambiguity often clouds discussions about whether morality is 'subjective' or 'objective'. These two words have almost as many senses as there are people who use them, and I shall not attempt to clear up all the obscurities here. But at least this much can be said. Whether or not someone is to blame for acting as he did is a subjective matter, in the sense that it will depend on his state of mind—how he saw his action, and whether he *thought* it right or wrong. On the other hand, whether what he did was the right thing to have done is an objective matter. It does not matter what the person thought; what matters is what was actually done, and how things actually turned out. Morality is concerned with both these questions, and so, from different points of view, morality is both subjective and objective.

25

That is all very well, and contributes something to clarity, I hope. But other important issues remain unresolved. Both sides in the debate seem to me to overstate their cases. On the 'conscience' side, the impression can be given that one's conscience is somehow an automatic source of *truth*—a kind of special faculty which homes unerringly in upon what is the right thing to do. Even Vatican II can give this impression in saying that in his conscience 'a man is alone with God whose voice echoes in its depths.' No doubt, what is echoing in the depths of someone's conscience *may* be the voice of God, and one *can* be alone with God there. But one might very well be alone simply with oneself, and the voice of conscience be simply the voice of one's prejudices, or those of the society in which one was brought up. 'Conscience' is not the name of some privileged insight with which we were all endowed at birth and which functions quite happily ever afterwards. It is simply the name of our ability to reflect intelligently on moral matters. Like any other ability, conscience needs to be nurtured and developed, and is quite capable of being stunted or warped. Our judgements of conscience are no more infallible than our judgements about anything else. Fidelity to one's conscience will ensure blamelessness and sincerity; but sincerity is no substitute for truth.

Similarly, those on the 'authority' side seem to assume that there is a very simple and direct connection between authority and truth. But we know that this connection is not always there at all, and even when it is there, it is often far from being simple and direct. In the case of human authorities, the difficulty is obvious enough. But at least some of these difficulties remain even with the authority of the Church, or the authority of the Bible. Neither the Church nor the Bible totally escapes all human limitations. The Church consists of human beings, and the response of the Church to the Holy Spirit is the response of human beings who are sometimes sinful, and always limited in their knowledge and outlook. In the same way, the Bible was written by men who used their own human minds and skills in writing it; it is precisely these minds and skills which the Spirit uses to lead men to God. Neither in the case of the Church nor in the case of the Bible can we see the guidance of God as somehow short-circuiting men's responses.

So it is perfectly possible for the Church to be mistaken on moral issues, as it was in its condoning of slavery right up to the early years of the nineteenth century. And even in those cases where the Church has been right (say, for the sake of argument, in its belief that some wars in the Middle Ages could be just wars) it is not a simple and direct matter to decide what that teaching should mean for us. It does not *simply* follow that some modern wars can also be just, and it may not even be true. Our Christian forefathers inevitably reflected the culture and outlook of their times, and they judged as best they could about their world as they saw it, with slaves and Crusades, monarchies and heathens. To learn from them, as we should, and to accept in general terms the authoritativeness of our tradition, does not by any means solve our problems about what precisely we should learn, or precisely in what respects they saw aright, if and when they did. Nor, as we have seen in the last chapter, does our belief in the authoritativeness of the New Testament make it any easier for us to be clear about precisely what it is that the New Testament has to teach us. The same goes for our Christian contemporaries in the Church of today. To recognize the authority of the Church is neither to say that everything said by the Church is true, nor that, even when it is true, it will be easy for us to see what can be learnt from it.

The same point can be put from the point of view of the bishops of the Church, whose task it is to discover and promote sound teaching in faith and morals. Where are *they* to look for such teaching, and how are they to identify it? We have already seen that they cannot solve their problem simply by saying to people 'Follow your consciences.' That is no guarantee of truth, and to say no more than that would be an abdication of responsibility. Neither can they simply repeat the sayings of Jesus or the teachings of previous Christian tradition, for the reasons we have already considered. Nor can they appeal to their own authority—for that will not help them to decide what they should authoritatively say. Where, then, are they to look?

One tempting answer is that they should look to the beliefs of the Church as a whole—what is called the *sensus fidelium*. In a way, this makes very good sense. Christ promised to be with the Church—the whole body of believers. And, in human terms, while individuals may be wrong about many things, it is less likely that everybody should be wrong about something, especially something which is of importance in their Christian lives. But this approach is still not enough. It is not so easy to say when such a consensus exists, and exactly about what, and it is particularly hard to find a consensus on something very specific. Thus, there might be a general consensus of all Christians that all human beings are equal in the sight of God and that unfair discrimination between them is contrary to Christian morality. But agreement will rapidly fade when one asks specific questions about equal voting rights, or wage differentials, or the legitimacy of capitalism in a Christian society. Christians might well agree about the sanctity of human life, and still differ widely in their views about capital punishment or pacifism.

Perhaps, then, sound moral teaching is to be looked for from those who are best acquainted with the issues in question? The bishops should ask married people about marriage, doctors about medical ethics, economists about social justice, and those living in the Third World about how we should try to help them? Here again, there is a great deal to be said for this approach, with its stress on first-hand experience and scholarly and scientific knowledge. But experts can disagree, and those most involved in a problem do not necessarily see clearest. Academic moralists are in danger of losing contact with 'grass-roots' experience of the Christian life in all its variety, and the ordinary Christian is apt to assume uncritically that his deepest moral convictions must surely reflect the will of God.

Perhaps this problem about where to look for sound teaching seems so difficult because it is being somehow approached from the wrong angle. I do not think that any resolution of the dilemma in this chapter is going to be totally satisfactory. But perhaps some tentative comments and suggestions can be made, despite the difficulties we have encountered.

First, are we perhaps unnecessarily anxious because we are looking for too much? The Holy Spirit, we believe, guides the Church in such a way that its members cannot fail to be led to their salvation if they choose to be. But, so far as morals is concerned, just how much guidance *is* required for our salvation? Surely we do not require correct answers to all our moral problems—that would be too much for any human mind. To be sure, we would reasonably expect the Church to help all its members to remain sensitive to the whole range of moral ideals—the sanctity of life, the ideals of marriage, forgiveness, social justice and so on. But I think it unreasonable to expect in a pilgrim Church that everything will be clear. We are surely able to trust that the Lord will not mark all our iniquities at least at the point where our limited human minds have gone as far as they can.

Secondly, it is important for the Church as a body to consider how it presently seeks for the truth in moral matters. If we cannot expect to have all the answers, at the very least we can try to look for them in the right spirit, and with the right tools. It goes without saying that all of us should avoid rancour, denunciation and accusations of bad faith or disloyalty against those with whose views we disagree. No search for truth will make any progress in such an atmosphere. Then, I suspect that it may be important to concentrate less of our attention on the need to produce answers and on the tentative answers which seem to be emerging, and to focus instead on the methods of argument and research which go into the discussion. Instead of rushing to see what conclusions a person reaches so that we can applaud or condemn, it might be better to see what arguments and methods he has used, so that if we applaud it will be for the right reasons, and if we disagree some constructive progress might nonetheless be made. Apart from that, it is surely right that the Christian community should foster not merely the widest possible consultation, but also the most open discussion of contentious moral problems. At the specialist level of academic debate, we could at least expect that a debate conducted in all freedom and rigour might at least identify the precise points of disagreement, and might arrive at some method by which they could be further explored. At a less academic level, everyone can be encouraged to ask themselves what they really do believe about moral issues, and to express their views. Documents published for general discussion, such as have already appeared on marriage, the right to strike and several aspects of medical ethics, which do not attempt to be definitive statements, seem to me to be just the kind of thing that is wanted. We need, in short, to foster the kind of Christian community in which it is recognized that we need to grow in truth, and in which each of us is prepared actively to encourage anyone who honestly tries to do so.

So far, I have been stressing the need for our own intellectual and personal efforts in moral reflection—our side of co-operation with the Spirit of God. My final suggestion is that we need to imitate Jesus' practice of praying to the Father. I say this not because I expect the results of such prayer to be any blinding flash of moral insight or an instant solution to all our dilemmas, but because I think it is of great importance for our attitude as Christians to moral reflection. To pray seriously is to admit to ourselves our need for a genuine openness to God; it is to express a willingness to be moved in whatever direction he would have us go; it requires of us that we be detached even from our most dearly held theories and arguments, and that we be willing to love and learn from even our most severe critics. Such an openness to God in prayer is what can give us confidence that our efforts to think about morality will not be ours alone, but the efforts of a pilgrim Church led by the Spirit of God.

INTERLUDE

We may now take stock of what we can learn from the various positions we have been considering.

I hope it will be clear how futile it is simply to reiterate any of these positions simply as it stands. None of them can claim to be a satisfactory account of how a Christian should approach moral questions. Some of these views are true, but true only of one aspect of moral thinking. Others are in part true and in part misleading. Others again are based on presuppositions which simply do not hold good, so that a thorough recasting of the issues has to be done before any progress can be made.

I have tried to show in what ways it is possible to advance beyond the blunt alternatives with which we started. Specifically, I think we can take the following positions as a starting point for our further exploration.

(1) For a Christian, the full meaning and beauty of the moral life will appear only in the light of his Christian faith. This faith will demand of him the fullest commitment to living a morally good life as part of the integral preaching of the Gospel. On the other hand, the arguments which the Christian will use to discover what the moral life requires should be arguments which can be fully shared with any human being.

(2) Our vocation in Christ is to try to respond to the demands of our world as well as he did to his. But to learn from him and from the rest of our tradition we need to do more than slavishly copy his actions or repeat previous teachings word for word. Only to the extent that we have some moral understanding of our own, in our own world, will we be able to understand the moral worlds of our Christian past and learn from them.

(3) To walk blamelessly before God, we must follow our conscience by fearlessly and honestly doing our duty as we see it to be. To be sensible, we should all recognize the value, and on occasions the necessity, of seeking and taking authoritative advice

in our moral lives. On the other hand, neither conscience nor authority can always guarantee truth. To grow towards the truth in God, we need a particular kind of community and a particular style of moral research and debate.

The main point to emerge from all three chapters is the need to develop the main outlines of what a method of moral argument should look like. We need to know how to avoid some of the mistakes and pitfalls in moral discussion. The second part of this book will consist in an attempt to construct at least a basic framework for moral thinking.

PART TWO

A FRAMEWORK FOR CHRISTIAN MORALITY

4

CHRISTIAN MORALITY AS FULFILMENT

The Aim and Scope of Christian Morality
Christians believe that Jesus of Nazareth was fully and perfectly man, like us in all things except sin. What are the implications of this belief for the Christian concept of morality? The most important consequence of this view is that Christians have a particular view of God. The God of the Christian faith is a God whose goodness can be revealed in a human life; and conversely, the Christian sees humanity as capable of revealing God, and the growth towards perfect humanity as being also a growth in the understanding of God. Of course, only in Jesus are human perfection and the revelation of God complete and perfect. But because we are members of Christ's body, and called to be adopted sons of God in Christ, it is also true of us that to the extent that our human lives are truly human, truly fulfilled, we too will be signs of the presence of the Kingdom whose completeness is yet to come. To the extent that we understand what human fulfilment consists in, we will come to understand God's eternal plan in creating us in the way he did. The Christian view of moral growth, then, is at once a view of human fulfilment and of the revelation of God in our lives. Progress in Christian morality will, therefore, be based on an understanding of our true needs as men and women.

Before we go on to consider what our true needs are, perhaps it is worth forestalling a possible objection to this whole line of approach. It might be asked, what is the use of trying to base morality on human fulfilment when we know that fulfilment is not possible in this life anyway? Would it not be more realistic to see this life as a dying to self, in order to rise again perfected in the next? In short, fulfilment is for the next life, and morality in this should be guided by the image of Christ's Cross?

It must be admitted that the person who lives a morally good life in this world will not necessarily live a life of fulfilment. To begin with, we can all fall prey to accident or illness, to premature bereavement, to any of the misfortunes that flesh is heir to. It would be idle to pretend that these ills do nothing to impede our human fulfilment. Again, the good man can fall victim not only to natural disasters, but to the ill-deeds of others. Sometimes he can be persecuted by others precisely because he is a good man, as Jesus himself was. A life which ended in misunderstanding, rejection, and death on the Cross cannot be described as a life of human fulfilment in any straightforward sense. The problem of evil is a real one, not to be glibly dismissed as an illusion which will disappear if we look at it in the light of faith. Christian tradition had made great efforts to understand how evil and sin can still be brought under the providence of God, and has developed the theology of the Cross, of sacrifice, of death and resurrection, in order to try to make the mystery of sin and evil somehow intelligible, or, if not intelligible, at least bearable. It *is* a matter of faith that Christ has triumphed over the evil in the world.

But it would be a perverse theology of the Cross to think of suffering as a good thing to be sought after, or which sees a life of frustration and suffering as a necessary prelude to the happiness of heaven. Jesus himself prayed that it might not be so in his own life. If suffering is inevitable then it must be faced, as Jesus faced it. But it is part of our Christian belief that if only we can ourselves succeed in living as we ought, and helping others to live as they ought, evil is not inevitable, and suffering can be minimized. It is part of our Christian faith that even in this life we can glimpse enough of what human fulfilment is like to make some sense of the final fulfilment which God has promised us. This is the aim of a Christian morality.

The framework of a Christian morality must therefore consist in a method for discovering where our true needs lie, for it is in satisfying our true needs that our fulfilment is to be found. Of course, the moral life is more than thinking and reflection—it requires action. Consequently moral development requires more than the growth in our powers of moral reasoning. It requires also the development of virtue—an emotional commitment to back up our moral choices. Ideally, we should feel inclined to do what we know we ought to do. In this section, however, I shall be concentrating on the intellectual side of our moral development. Where are our moral judgements likely to go wrong?

From Wants to True Needs

Since the Christian view of man is truly a humanism, it is possible for the Christian to conduct his search for true human needs along lines which he can share with any human being. Where, then, is the search to start?

I suggest that the only place to start looking for what we truly need is by looking at the things we say we want. Of course we know very well that we do not truly need all the things we say we want, and it would be absurd to suggest that human fulfilment consists in everyone getting everything they think they want. If it is true that our wants are the evidence for our true needs, it is also true that the evidence will need to be sifted and carefully evaluated. Yet we must also be careful not simply to dismiss some wants as bad just because of our existing moral preconceptions—for it may be those preconceptions which themselves need to be rejected. What is needed is some comparatively neutral grounds on which we can criticize the wants we have without making too many moral assumptions right at the start.

It will help to think for a moment about how we come to want things in the first place. By the very fact that we are human beings, we start off our lives with a particular set of urges and drives which distinguish us from, say, pythons or gorillas. It is hard to say exactly what these urges and drives are. None of us can remember them in their 'primitive' stages, and to put names to them is already to interpret them to a certain extent. Still, we may say roughly that they concern such things as food, physical well-being, sex, affection, a role in society, knowledge. From our very earliest days, we learn to translate these very general drives into particular desires for this or that or the next thing. The particular wants that we have will depend not just on the general drives which we share with all human beings, but also on the culture and society in which we are brought up. We *learn* what to want, through an interplay between our basic human drives and what we are told is good for us by others. So, I have learnt to want to listen to classical music, and other people have not. Young people in the West have learnt to want to choose whom they shall marry; in other cultures they have learnt to want to marry someone chosen as suitable by their parents and families. Some people have learnt to want TV, or drugs, or evening classes in theology or a week in Benidorm. Some families have learnt to want to express their affection for one another in a physically demonstrative way; others have learnt to want just the opposite. And so on, in amazing variety.

It would be a mistake to think that all the wants we have learnt must inevitably be selfish. Of course, someone *can* learn to be selfish; but we need not learn this. It is possible (and, I would hope, more normal) for people to learn to want to help one another, to be honest, to be passionately concerned about justice. So we need not fear that if we base a morality on the wants we have, that morality will inevitably end up as a morality of self-seeking. Still, what can be learnt can also be badly learnt. We can learn a pattern of wants, satisfying which will as a matter of fact damage ourselves or others rather than fulfil us.

Drug-addicts or psychopathic killers are particularly striking examples of this, but possessive lovers or the compulsively shy or habitual liars are just more everyday examples of the same kind of thing. So we need some way of discriminating between all the wants we have learnt so as to discern that pattern of wants which will point us towards our true fulfilment as individuals and as members of a human society. How is this to be done? Which wants are likely to be truly fulfilling?

Wants Based on True Information

We want many things only because we have made a mistake about something else. A person can set his heart on going to a university in the mistaken belief that he has the ability to profit from study there. Two people might want to get married, when all their friends can see quite clearly that they are totally unsuited to each other and will never be able to make each other happy. A parent might wish for a very protected environment for his children because he believes that to protect them for as long as possible is to give them a better chance in life. I might be unwilling to see a doctor because I do not realise that there is anything seriously the matter with me. Typically, when such mistakes come to light we find ourselves saying, 'If only I had known, if only I had realized at the time!' Sometimes such mistakes have very serious consequences, sometimes less so; sometimes, even, we might be lucky and do very well out of our mistakes. But at least we can say this: a general policy of satisfying wants based on mistaken information is likely to cause damage, hurt and frustration for ourselves and others. The same holds good for larger issues as well as for more personal ones. The Chancellor might adopt an economic policy on the basis of expert advice which turns out to have been mistaken; millions of people might suffer as a result. Well-meaning people tried to help the Third World to industrialize as quickly as possible without understanding the problems which high technology brings in its train; in consequence, their efforts often did more harm than good.

The first step towards improving our moral choices, then, is to try as far as possible to base them on correct information. And the first moral habit we need to acquire is a willingness to revise our wants in the light of such information. It is fatally easy to think we know all we need to know when making moral decisions, stubbornly refusing to find out anything more, or even to listen to fresh facts when they are presented to us. Especially if we have adopted some moral stance in public, it is hard to bring ourselves to ask honestly what effect it is having, and whether the reasons we gave for it still hold good in the light of further experience. What is fatal is to suggest that experience has nothing to teach us about matters of moral principle. If we are going to say that something is wrong, then we must show, on the basis of experience, that it does someone harm, and the belief that it does harm must itself be supported with evidence. It will not do to make such assertions simply as undefended dogmas. If we are to say that something is good, then we must similarly show that it leads people to their fulfilment. It is not enough to say that it does because we wish that it did. It is no use John's *saying* that for him to marry Joan will lead to a life of fulfilment for them both; the question is, will it or will it not? In this sense, moral decisions need to be based on the best information that we can obtain, and questioned in the light of whatever further information might call them into doubt. Our moral decisions and our principles can be no better, and may be worse, than the factual information on which they should be based.

Wants which Form a Coherent Pattern of Life

There are times when all of us want to have our cake and eat it. Sometimes we try to hide the conflict from ourselves even when we know it is there; at other times, we may not realize that it just will not be possible to have both the things we want. So a man might try to convince himself that his career ambitions are perfectly compatible with his marriage. A student might want to pass his exams and also want to avoid spending time at lectures or in the library. A nation might want to have both full employment and a stable currency. Or again, things we might want now may be incompatible with what we know we will want later. Do we spend money now, or put it by for our retirement?

Just because our wants conflict in this way, it does not follow that we do not truly need each of the things we want. If that were so, the problem would be comparatively simple—we should simply abandon whichever want does not represent a true need. The real difficulty arises when each of the two needs is a perfectly legitimate need, but when there is no possible way in which both can be satisfied. If we just try to pretend to ourselves that we can continue to pursue each of our goals, we are in effect trying to produce the impossible, and that is not a rational thing to do. Something has to give. Either we must abandon one of our wants altogether, or we have to modify each of them in such a way that they can both be satisfied.

I am not here making any proposals about how such a choice should be made. I do not wish to exclude the possibility that someone faced with such a choice might prefer to give up very many of the things he wants in order to pursue just one important goal in his life. I see no way of proving either that it is wrong for someone to sacrifice a great deal in order to become a Carthusian monk, or a concert pianist, or a Nobel prizewinner in physics, or that it would be wrong for him not to make this sacrifice. It seems to me that human fulfilment can be found in many different ways of life, and that one and the same individual could be happy in several different vocations. All I wish to argue is that it will prove self-defeating, and ultimately unfulfilling, to conduct one's life as if such decisions do not have to be made. If morality is concerned with fulfilment, it requires us to develop a pattern of goals in our lives which can be realized.

Correctly Identified Wants

Unfortunately, we do not always know what we want. A comparatively trivial example of this can be seen in those occasions when we fidget around the the house feeling vaguely ill at ease. We try various ways of pinning down what is the matter—a good book, or some fresh air, or a cup of coffee, or a phone call to a friend. If after all these we still feel dissatisfied, we know that we have not yet succeeded in identifying what we really wanted. Sometimes the malaise can be much more serious. My whole life may come to seem empty, lacking an essential ingredient which I cannot pin down. Is my marriage not what it should be? Am I in the wrong kind of job, perhaps? Or living in the wrong place? Or just not getting enough relaxation, or enough variety, or something?

The difficulties are compounded when our wants are bound up with other people's. It may be hard enough for someone to say exactly what he is asking of a friendship, or in what ways he would like it to develop; it will be doubly hard if he does not know how the other person would answer that question. Especially in this kind of situation, there is the temptation to rest content with some agreed formula, even when it is clear that it does not really meet the case.

Pursuing wants which misrepresent our real needs is a recipe for frustration and unhappiness. Yet it is so easy to settle into a way of life which takes such inadequate goals for granted, simply because the alternative may be an uncomfortable reappraisal of ourselves which might in turn face us with some very unpalatable choices indeed.

Growth in Moral Judgement

The basis of correct moral decision, then, are those wants of ours which are based on correct information, form a coherent pattern of life, and correctly identify our desires, for it is on such wants alone that our fulfilment depends. A moment's reflection should make it plain that these apparently simple requirements are in fact extremely far-reaching. Taken together, they provide a powerful set of criteria for making a moral assessment of our existing wants and desires. Space does not permit me to show how they might be applied in detail to the whole range of problems confronting us in our moral lives, though I have tried to give some examples as I went along. The reader might like to take them as the basis for analysing whatever moral issues he is most interested in.

Two points should be made to guard against possible misunderstanding. Of course, it is true that none of us will ever be able to have all the correct information on which our wants should rest; we will not be aware of all the hidden incompatibilities between the goals that we set ourselves; and we will always to some extent lack that clarity of perception of our own deepest needs which we should like to have. We cannot suppose that we will succeed in avoiding all the pitfalls in our moral thinking to which these three criteria call attention. The most we can do, I think, is to set out the guidelines along which progress is to be made. Secondly, the true needs which we might discover along these lines are only the basis of morality. They tell us only which features of ourselves and others are relevant to the moral decisions we have to make. They do not, as the next section will make clear, provide all the data needed to solve our moral problems.

Still, they do provide a basic framework both for our own moral reflections and for a theory of moral education. They are initial guidelines for growth. We can regard them as a set of skills which we need to develop in order to think properly about moral issues and the lives we lead. The first skill is an analytic one. It consists in being able to see on what factual information our moral opinions depend, with a view to making sure that that information is as complete as it can reasonably be made. The second is the development of our ability to see where the incompatibilities in our life lie, and exactly which of our desires lie behind them. The third is more a matter of imagination, discernment and sympathy. A good deal of our failure to identify the sources of malaise or unhappiness in our lives stems from the inability to imagine real alternative ways of looking at ourselves and others. It is as if we were trying to see which shoe would really fit, and simply did not have enough shoes available to try on. Behind all these skills must lie the basic virtue of moral honesty—a genuine willingness to seek for the truth and to face it when it has been found. Without this honesty, the impulse towards moral growth will simply not be there.

Of course, as I have already remarked, moral growth involves more than growth in moral judgement. It requires a willingness to act on the moral judgements one makes, and that is a matter of emotional maturity, self-control and moral integrity. I have not directly considered this aspect of moral growth at all. Indirectly, however, it seems to me that what I have said has some bearing on our moral practice as well as on our moral thinking. It might be easier to live morally if we were clear about what the point of living morally was. On the picture of Christian moral thinking which I have presented, morality is a programme for discovering where our true fulfilment lies. It is not some list of external commands and prohibitions devised by God as a set of more or less arbitrary 'tests' in this life rewarded by happiness in the next. Such a picture of morality seems both philosophically objectionable, and profoundly unchristian. It can also have the unfortunate effect of undermining our moral motivation, even to the extent of fomenting a mood of rebellion against the moral life itself. Our motivation can be helped by a theory which presents God as willing us to find and live by what is truly best in ourselves.

Justice

On the basis of true needs, we can begin to build the final parts of the framework of Christian moral thinking. What are our moral duties?

The simplest and most direct way of doing this would be to say that our duty is to try to satisfy the true needs of as many people as possible. To love one another as ourselves is to be willing to work for everyone's fulfilment, to the best of our limited insight and abilities. Unfortunately, this simple and direct solution will not prove entirely adequate; and, even more unfortunately, it is not entirely clear how a fully adequate account is to be given.

First, though, let us see how far the simple theory will take us. It will do very well for all those situations in which the fulfilment of one person presents no obstacle to the fulfilment of others. Often enough, it will be true that one person can be truly happy only if those around him also are. A family is perhaps the most obvious example of this. It may be a hard lesson to learn that our happiness does not really lie in exploiting or manipulating those closest to us, but it is a true lesson for all that. Furthermore, situations in which it appears that one person, or group of persons, can be truly happy and fulfilled only at the expense of others can perhaps be transformed into situations in which there is no such conflict. A simple example can illustrate this. Suppose that he wants a mountaineering holiday which she couldn't stand, while she wants to laze on a sunny beach, which would bore him to tears. The solution might appear to be that no holiday could satisfy them both. But a better solution might be found by remembering that our wants have been learnt, and it is possible that they can be re-learnt at least to some extent. Even if neither of them has ever tried it before, it might be that he could find in a sailing holiday the element of physical challenge which he enjoys, while she might find

42

it sufficiently restful and relaxing to satisfy her as well. The same kind of point can be made in much more serious cases. It seems true that all of us in the developed world have learnt a set of needs which can be satisfied only at the expense of those in the underdeveloped world, and, in the case of the use of scarce resources such as energy, only at the expense of our children and our children's children. Yet it may be possible to find some other pattern of needs which we could learn, and satisfying which would truly fulfil us, without our fulfilment having been attained at the expense of others.

In short, the simple theory will urge us to satisfy the needs of as many people as possible, and to re-learn our needs in such a way as to make them compatible with the true needs of others. Just as it is morally wrong to ignore others' needs, it is morally wrong to learn ways of fulfilling ourselves at the expense of others, when we could equally learn to be fulfilled in harmony with the fulfilment of others. So far, so good.

The real problems arise when there is simply no way available of enabling everyone to live a fulfilled life—say, because resources of food, or energy or health care are so scarce that it is quite inevitable that someone must suffer genuine deprivation. A similar problem arises for us also in situations in which, while there might in theory be some way of satisfying everyone, we are quite unable to see what it is. Thus, for example, there might be a way of so running the economy that everyone can have a decent wage, a job which is meaningful and useful, and an adequate provision for his health and the education and welfare of his family. But if we are unable to devise such an economic strategy, it is inevitable that someone will suffer genuine deprivation. It is at this point that it would be desirable to have an adequate theory of justice. I take it that the point of a theory of justice is to give us some way of deciding who shall suffer, and to what extent, given that it is inevitable that some suffering there must be.

For such cases of genuine extremity there is, so far as I know, no generally accepted solution. To put it bluntly, is it more just that everyone should gradually starve to death, or is it more just that some should have enough, and the rest starve much more quickly? And if the first solution, for all its egalitarian attractiveness, seems unnecessarily wasteful in terms of human lives, the second, which at least enables some to survive, presents almost insuperable problems about how to choose those who are to be so favoured.

In less extreme cases, perhaps some partial solution is available. One might say that where resources are scarce, our duty is first to those who are most seriously deprived. We might also look for forms of deprivation which are at least less radically dehumanizing, and try to avoid those which are most dehumanizing. Ultimately, however, it

43

seems to me that our moral theory is at this point inadequate. Or, to put it in theological terms, it is at this point that moral theory confronts the problem of evil, and we can do no more than trust that the wisdom of God can finally triumph over our human inadequacies.

Two Practical Illustrations
Two reasonably typical cases of moral perplexity will serve to illustrate how moral reflection according to this pattern might proceed in practice.

A Domestic Problem
John and Susan are married with three children. Susan's father has just died, leaving her elderly mother living 200 miles away, with no other close relatives. John and Susan are considering whether they ought to insist that she come to live with them. They feel that otherwise she might find things too much for her, and they are afraid that she might fall ill, with nobody around to help. Mother, on the other hand, says that she will be perfectly all right, and that she has no intention of moving.

The reader may possibly feel somewhat let down by the very ordinariness of this example. He will shortly discover that the points I will make about it are also perfectly ordinary, even obvious, points. If this is all that Christian moral reflection amounts to, he might wonder, what is all the fuss about? Yet the very homely and ordinary nature of this example is important, for this reason: it cannot be too strongly emphasized, I believe, that the vast majority of moral perplexities *are* ordinary. It would be most unfortunate if the impression were given that morality was concerned only with the spectacular or the sensational, or was restricted to only one or two areas of human concern. Any situation in which the fulfilment and well-being of human persons is involved is a morally significant situation; and most of these situations have nothing sensational about them at all. Nor is there anything highly sophisticated about how we should go about reflecting in such situations. Most of us engage in moral reflection of one kind or another every day of our lives, without there being anything dramatic about it. I think it is important for us to recognize that we are *already* very good at moral reflection. We already know how to do it, at least in general terms. If a more controversial issue comes along (and to some extent my second example will illustrate this), it is not a matter of suddenly trying to think in a way totally different from our ordinary

44

one; it is a matter simply of not losing our nerve, and continuing to approach things as we usually do.

In the light of the moral framework set out earlier in this chapter, then, how would this domestic problem be approached? The general policy will be first of all to get more information about the situation. In particular, we will need information about how well the people involved have identified what they really want: we will need to know whether any of their views depend on mistaken beliefs; and we will need to know where, if at all, their real needs conflict.

What do the people really want? Take Mother, for example. She says that she wants to stay where she is, and that she is much happier in her own house, with her own neighbours. Of course, this might be perfectly true. Equally, however, she might have several more complicated feelings. Her desire to stay where she is might be coloured by her fear that she would not really be welcome at John and Susan's and that she would only be in the way. If she knew that they really did want to have her, she might, deep down, much prefer to go and live with them, rather than be all on her own. Again, she might think that she will be quite happy to carry on more or less as she did when her husband was alive. But it is also possible that her desire to be brave and practical prevents her from seeing that she really needs company, which she would no longer have if she were to stay on as she is. Susan, meanwhile, believes that she would prefer to have her mother with her. Perhaps she truly does want this: but perhaps, too, her conventional belief that she *ought* to want this blinds her to the fact that she would resent her mother's daily presence, and would not want her to be on the spot to see all the details of how she and John run their home.

There are also more emotionally neutral matters of fact which need to be clarified. The proposed move might involve converting an attic into an extra room, which John and Susan mistakenly believe they are able to afford only because they have not actually checked up to find out how much it would cost to have it done. John and Susan might also believe that Mother will easily make new friends among their neighbours, and that she will adapt easily to her new surroundings. But possibly Mother's former versatility in this respect has lessened somewhat with her advancing years, and she in fact will not be able to settle in comfortably? Or, to take the example in the other direction, John and Susan might agree to Mother's staying where she is because they imagine that she is in excellent health for her age. In fact, had they only known, she might be far from well, and they should after all have insisted that she move to where they could be near her.

There are also possible conflicts between the various needs which must be considered. For example, perhaps Mother wants to move, and Susan wants to have her, but having her might introduce tensions into the home which nobody wants. It might prove impossible to be fair to the children and to Mother, if only because she needs a degree of predictable peace and quiet which is impossible in a household containing three teenagers. Again, Susan might consider that if Mother does come she herself will have to give up her job; and that, in turn, might have serious financial implications for the family as a whole. Mother herself might have to choose between her fear of loneliness and her fear of being a burden on others. John might have to choose between his desire to be generous and considerate and his feeling of awkwardness with Mother who seems to make him irritable and some-how possessive towards Susan.

I hope that by now it is evident that in any such situations the issues will not be entirely clear cut. Depending on how all these questions are answered, there may well be various possible courses of action each of which has a good deal to be said both for and against it. It must not be assumed that there is always one clearly correct answer to every moral problem, still less that moral theologians exist to provide such an answer. It is perfectly possible that more than one answer would be reasonable, given the information available and our limited insight into ourselves and others. Divergence of moral opinion should not of itself surprise or disturb us. Nor do professional moralists have some specially privileged insight which will yield better answers in every case. The most that can be expected of the moralist is that he be able to point out which features of such cases are likely to be relevant, and to be able, if need be, to integrate his approach to this case into a more general theory of Christian moral living. Yet, as I have argued earlier, it is not enough for anyone just to say, 'They must reach their own decision.' Of course they must. But that does nothing to help them to consider what makes for a good decision, and what they should think about in coming to their decision. I have suggested that a decision will be the better for having taken into account all the elements in the situation which have a bearing on the well-being and fulfilment of all the people involved. To insist on the objectivity of morality is to insist that all these factors be carefully weighed, for an objective morality is concerned with what actually happens to people—happens as a matter of objective fact, so to speak—and not with what we think might happen, or would like to believe would happen.

As I have presented the example thus far, authorities have played no role in the matter at all. It is not hard to see what role they could play. Susan might, for example, talk over the whole decision with a friend of hers who once was faced with a similar problem, and who now has considerable experience of how it all worked out in practice.

46

If Susan and John are totally unable to decide what would be best, they might simply take Susan's friend's advice without further question, though that would surely be an unusual and extreme case. More normally, they might find the advice helpful and illuminating, but would also be aware that their friend's mother and Susan's mother are two different people, and one cannot simply treat the one as if she were the other. Susan and John will have to consider how far their friend's advice is relevant and how far it is not. Even good authorities have to be followed with intelligent judgement.

Specifically Christian authorities on this kind of problem are rather difficult to find. To be sure, the commandments require us to honour our parents, and the great commandment of Christ requires us to love others as we love ourselves. One might perhaps point out that several passages in the Old Testament suggest that grandparents normally lived with their children. But clearly none of this is decisive. The Old Testament merely reflects the ordinary social structure of the time, and cannot be assumed to apply automatically to the very different social structures of our own day. It would be absurd to suggest that the only way in which John and Susan can love and honour Mother is by having her to live with them. Christian tradition, then, provides John and Susan with no line of solution which would not equally be available to their non-Christian friends. Yet the whole weight of that tradition surely urges them to take this decision as seriously and unselfishly as they can; what following Christ requires of them is that they be willing to use all their honesty, sensitivity and intelligence to try to discover what really would be for the best for everyone concerned.

The End of a Marriage?

In the previous example, Christian moral reflection required a serious concern for the well-being of the people involved, and an intelligent use of the various authorities who might throw light on the issue. I suggest that exactly the same considerations are important in this second example. It is not as if there are two quite different processes of Christian reflection, one for ordinary cases, and another reserved for more controversial or difficult cases. Consider the following situation.

David and Ann have been living together for the last three years, following the breakdown of David's marriage to Mary.

One view of the matter is that we can stop right there. The Christian view of the situation is quite simple, and clear in the tradition. The Commandments clearly forbid adultery; and the teaching of Jesus himself forbids divorce and remarriage as being no better than adultery. David and Ann are therefore sinning in that they are committing adultery. The situation certainly cannot be rectified by their getting married; indeed, they are obliged to split up, and David should return to Mary if that is at all possible.

On the other hand, the line of reflection which I have been advocating would certainly not stop there. It would proceed on exactly the same lines as in the previous case. On this approach, the first thing to notice is that the situation, as it has so far been described, is extremely unclear. Why, for example, have David and Ann not married? Is it that he has hopes of showing that his marriage to Mary was not a valid one, but is unwilling to marry Ann unless and until this has been shown? Or is it that he is locked into an affair with Ann largely because he cannot face the prospect of another relationship coming to nothing as his relationship with Mary did? Is it that Ann maintains that marriage is an outdated social convention which people who really love one another should be strong enough to do without? Or is it that David, having made, as he sees it, one serious mistake as a result of which he and Mary were both seriously hurt, is now unwilling to marry Ann until they are sure that this might not be a mistake too? In general, I suggest that both David and Ann, faced with such questions, might be far from clear about what each of them really wants—certainly much less clear than they would like to admit even to each other.

Besides, what of Mary? Does she still hope that David will one day come back, or is she quite happy that he has found someone with whom he has settled down at last? Has she herself remarried? In general, for all we so far know to the contrary, the needs of Mary and David and Ann might not really be as conflicting as they appear. It need not be true, for all we know, that David needs Ann and Mary needs David, and Ann also needs David. Perhaps David and Mary really do need each other after all, and Ann would be happier if only she were to marry someone quite different. Again, it might be that neither Mary nor David needs the other at all, but that David and Ann do. In which case, once again, there is no conflict of needs. Furthermore, nothing so far has been said about any children, and what their needs might be. Has Mary got children who badly need a father? Have David and Ann got children who need a more secure home than David and Ann, unmarried, can provide?

Again, there are questions of fact, over and above the desires of the people involved. Mary and David might want to reunite, but it might be asked whether, after all that has happened in the last three years, they still have the emotional resources to make it work. Mary might feel that she can bring up her children single handed; she might be correct in this belief, but she equally (for all we know) might not be.

Such questions could be multiplied almost indefinitely. The general point I wish to make is that it makes a considerable moral difference what the true answers to them are, for these answers have an important bearing on our estimate of the effect of any decision on the well-being of the people involved. If it is true that Christian ethics are based on a belief that God made us for our fulfilment, then any circumstance which affects people's fulfilment must be considered before a properly Christian decision can be reached. In this respect, this example is no different from the previous one.

Unlike the previous example, however, this case perhaps highlights the fact that we are often extremely reluctant even to ask the questions upon which a good decision should depend. We are all reluctant to admit that we have made mistakes, and even more reluctant to admit that we might be making one at the moment. We tend to shy away from any line of argument which might in the end require us to alter our present arrangements in any radical way. There is the temptation to rationalize our present conduct even in defiance of the true facts of the situation. The first thing that Christian morality requires is that such issues be squarely faced, in the light of all the known facts.

I think it is also important in cases of this kind to keep two different issues quite separate. One issue is whether, years ago, a wrong was done, and, if so, by whom; quite another issue is to ask what the people involved should now do. Thus, it might be quite true to say that David wronged Mary when he first became involved with Ann; but it does not at all follow that he is continuing to wrong her by remaining with Ann instead of going back to Mary. It might be that that is just what he ought to do, for everyone's sake. Suppose, for example, that the present situation is as follows: Mary has no children, but has remarried. David and Ann now have two children, and are happy. It would seem perverse to suggest that David and Mary have a duty to break up their second homes and go back to each other, leaving Ann to look after the children alone. Indeed, there would seem to be good reasons for wondering whether it is not high time that David and Ann got married in a registry office. This would be quite a different situation from one in which, for instance, Mary has been looking after David's children, and wants him back: David and Ann have no children, and no real commitment to each other; and the only reason David does not go back to Mary is a mixture of shame, pride and the fear that she does not really want him, or could not really forgive him.

That these two situations are so different (and there are many other possible variations which I have not considered) surely demonstrates

49

the falsity of the view that would have judged the situation as originally sketched out without seeing the need for any further inquiry at all. But that view was based on an important element in Christian tradition; and this tradition, going back to Jesus himself, should surely have an important bearing on any Christian decision which has to be made. The difficulty of this example, in contrast to the earlier ones, comes from the difficulty of fitting together a proper respect for Christian tradition and a regard for all the complexities of the case as it affects the individuals concerned. How is this to be done?

The first thing to do is to try to understand the tradition as accurately as possible. Precisely what was Jesus' own attitude to the Mosaic practice of allowing divorce provided the position of the women was legally safeguarded and she was not simply turned out of the house? Jesus said that the Mosaic law took into account the hard-heartedness of the Jews. Does Jesus believe that the Mosaic law was wrong to give in to people in this way? In that case, he might be saying that his disciples should not make that mistake. Or perhaps Jesus thought that the Mosaic tradition was right in taking the hard-heartedness of the people into account, but believed that his disciples, with their understanding of the Kingdom, would not be so hard hearted, and so concessions in their case would be unnecessary. Or again, he might have taken the view that, even if his disciples were hard hearted like their ancestors, it was still better for the law to put a higher ideal before them, without necessarily insisting on the full penalties of the law being inflicted on transgressors (witness his treatment of Mary Magdalen, and, perhaps, of the woman taken in adultery).

I have already pointed out that the community for whom Matthew's Gospel was written seems to have held that an exception to Jesus' teaching on divorce was to be made in the case of adultery. Some Christian Churches, notably in the East, have continued to accept the Matthaean version of the tradition. In the main, however (with the exception made to permit a believer married to a pagan to remarry a Christian, allegedly on the authority of St Paul), the Christian tradition has taken the stricter teaching of Jesus, and has enshrined that teaching in its law.

The origins of the tradition, then, are somewhat unclear, and subsequent generations have taken it in ways which are at least slightly different. But even on the weaker interpretation of Jesus' teaching, it is surely clear that he taught that the permanence of marriage was an ideal; and ideals, if they are to be of any value, must have some influence on actual practice. It would be dishonest to claim to follow an ideal which was never allowed to make any practical difference. What difference ought it to make, then?

Perhaps it is reasonable to suppose that the original teaching of

Jesus was given in the context of a discussion of Law. If so, it is possible to relate that teaching to our contemporary problems about the relationship between legislation and public morality. Legislation has an important function to perform for the community in the area of moral education, at least in those areas in which it possible to say that community as a whole endorses a shared moral outlook. And even in those areas where there is a wide divergence of moral view in the community, the Law has to take into account its effects on the well-being of the citizens. On the other hand, a law which is, or attempts to be, much stricter than the moral outlook of the community as a whole will be widely disregarded, and this in turn will bring the Law itself into disrepute. An example of this would be the legislation prohibiting the sale of alcohol in the United States in the twenties. Excessively restrictive legislation can be seriously counterproductive. Perhaps we can use our experience of such problems in our own day to throw light on the teaching of Jesus himself. If people's attitude to marriage is already very much more permissive, then to forbid divorce and remarriage might be counterproductive; better to make sure at least that divorce would be legally and properly carried out. Moses, as a wise legislator, took into consideration the hard-heartedness of his people. On the other hand, if people in general respect the permanence of marriage, it is no service to them if the Law does not reinforce this moral attitude; a law forbidding divorce would then have the effect of reminding them of their ideals. Such might have been Jesus' view of the situation in his own day, which would have been why he spoke as he did.

This account of the teaching of Jesus is inevitably somewhat speculative, as any attempt to reconstruct the precise point of our earliest traditions must be. Still, it would explain the sayings and practice of Jesus well, I think; and it would also explain why it was that the Matthaean community felt able to depart from the Master's teaching to some extent; it would have been judging what legislation would have the best effects in its own case. If this line of interpretation is correct, then the question which must be asked in the contemporary Church in the light of the tradition is this: what marriage legislation would most benefit the members of the Church, and would be most helpful in keeping before them the ideals of marriage without leading to ccunterproductive effects? This is, of course, a matter of judgement, and involves sociological factors of some complexity. It may even be that different parts of the contemporary Church would ideally need different legislation, as seems to have been the case in New Testament times on this and on a number of other issues. My own view, however, for what it is worth, is that at least for the Western Church it would be most unwise to alter our present laws on divorce and remarriage.

I would think that most Christians have a deep moral respect for the permanence of marriage, and that a strict law on the matter is therefore beneficial to us.

If that is right, then we can see more easily the bearing that the tradition ought to have on the decisions to be made in our example. For it follows that David and Ann could never remarry in the Church. On the other hand, we must remember that in saying this we are making a legal statement in the light of a general legal policy aimed at the well-being and fulfilment of the members of the Church as a body. We are not directly making a moral statement about what other duties David and Ann might have. As I have indicated, some versions of the original case might lead to the conclusion that it might be their moral duty to set up home in as permanent a manner as possible, to make each other and their children as happy and secure as they can. Whatever may have been the sins of their past, it might well be their duty now to provide a stable Christian home for each other and their children. If this is their duty, they should not in any sense be regarded as living in sin. Nevertheless, neither can the Church recognize this marriage as a Christian marriage in the legal sense, even while it encourages them to foster a Christian family life. It is one thing to argue for a particular legal policy for the welfare of the members of the Church; a separate, and equally important point is that the members of the Church have a duty to provide every possible pastoral means to help the couple foster their life as a Christian family.

It might be asked why, in that case, the Church ought not to alter its marriage law to conform more closely to the moral requirements of such situations? I think that the answer to this is that the Church has to balance the welfare of individual couples against the welfare of the community as a whole, whereas in this case there is a conflict between the two. The morality of the actions of the individual couple is determined by the effects of those actions on the people involved; but the morality of adopting a particular attitude in law must depend on much wider considerations involving the general welfare. That this general policy will bear hardly on individuals is simply a consequence of the fact that interests genuinely conflict. On the other hand, it is essential to this position to maintain a clear distinction between the legal position of such individuals, and a moral judgement upon them. And it is also essential that everything that can be done for them in Christian love should be done.

These two examples, in their different ways, will illustrate the general approach to Christian moral reflection. This approach demands a critical but sensitive acceptance of our Christian tradition, combined with an abiding willingness to remember that that tradition is based on God's will that human beings be truly fulfilled. I hope to have given some substance to the arguments of earlier chapters, by showing how a serious concern for the facts of human well-being can both illuminate our understanding of tradition, and help us to understand our own moral perplexities in the light of that tradition.

5

CHRISTIAN MORALITY FOR ALL MEN

A Universal Morality?
Will the kind of moral theory which we have outlined on the basis of
our true fulfilment and the twin duties of love and justice apply to
everyone alike? Does it leave any place for moral rules and universal
principles?

The view that a moral theory consists of universal moral principles
has had something of a bad press recently. Some would regard any
universal moral rule as an infringement on the liberty of the individual;
and some Christian writers would argue that to advocate moral rules
is to support just the very legalism that the Gospel should free us
from, and which Jesus himself so often criticized. I believe that both
these attacks on moral principles are misdirected, and that they stem
from a series of misunderstandings about the nature of moral principles, and the role they play in our moral lives.

The first point to be made is a quite general one, which follows
directly from what has been so far said. A moral rule is not a command, but a truth. Or, to be more accurate, since truth is not always
within our grasp, a moral principle sets out what we take to be a truth.
So a moral principle, for example, that is wrong to kill someone, is
not a command like 'Don't kill!', but a statement to the effect that
killing people impedes their fulfilment as human beings. Perhaps it is
the word 'Law', so often used in connection with moral principles,
which helps to foster this misunderstanding of moral principles as
commands. A parallel can be seen if we consider for a moment the
case of scientific laws. The law of gravity simply states what we take
to be a truth about the behaviour of bodies in certain circumstances.
It neither tells them how to behave, nor does it tell us how to behave.
We can, if we choose, take a running jump off the cliffs of Dover as
a cheap way of going to France for a holiday. The law of gravity does
not forbid us to do this; it simply states where and when we can expect
to splash down in the Channel. The law of gravity is not in any sense
a threat to our freedom of conscience, nor is it somehow a denial of
our right to the freedom of the children of God according to the
Gospel. It is just the same, I suggest, with our moral laws or principles.

Suppose we say that it is wrong to behave possessively towards others. All we are saying is that to behave in this way impedes our fulfilment and theirs. If this moral principle be true, it enables us to predict that damage will result from certain kinds of behaviour, just as the law of gravity enables us to predict where we will come down to earth if we jump off the cliffs of Dover. We can, if we so choose, ignore this moral principle in the way we act; but if the principle is a true one, we must realize that there will in fact be a price to be paid for so acting. This is a matter of fact, just as the force of gravity is. To resent it as a threat to our freedom is just as absurd in the one case as it would be in the other.

Presenting moral principles as commands by speaking of them in terms of obedience, imperatives and so on, has the unfortunate consequence of provoking an equally unjustified reaction in terms of freedom of conscience, the liberties of the individual, and even Gospel instead of Law. An equally unfortunate consequence is that the connection between moral principles, the evidence in terms of which they must be supported, and the truths which they purport to express, is completely obscured. It is most regrettable that those who most wish to stress the importance of having moral principles to live by are so often those who exhibit least concern to show on what facts the truth of such principles rests. If it is true that, for example, pre-marital sex is wrong, it must be because engaging in that activity impedes people's fulfilment. If the energy expended on reiterating the principle were to be spent instead on showing how and why and in what circumstances such damage occurs, one might hope that the principle itself would be more widely believed.

The first function of our moral principles, then, is to present the truth as we see it about the relationship between types of behaviour and human fulfilment. It follows, I think, that our moral principles will be open to correction in the light of further evidence. For example, if there is evidence that capital punishment does not serve as an effective deterrent to serious crime, then that knowledge should make us willing to alter our moral view that capital punishment is morally permissible.

There is another slightly different role which moral principles can play in our moral thinking. They may not set out to express the full complexity of our moral beliefs on a particular point, but simply to remind us of some particularly important aspects of those beliefs. Take for example the principle that it is wrong to break promises. I take this principle to express our belief that it is a good thing for society that people keep the promises they have made, and that, in the end, all of us benefit from being able to rely on people's word in this way. In short, to break a promise is an undesirable thing in itself.

In an older terminology, promise-breaking is intrinsically wrong. It is wrong just because it is the kind of behaviour it is. On the other hand, none of us believes that that is all there is to be said on the subject. We are well aware that there are quite a few occasions on which promises have to be broken. Our knowledge on this point is quite complex, as will become evident if one tries to spell out exactly when one would think it justifiable or even obligatory to break a promise. Still, the value of the principle is that it serves as a constant reminder that, although it is not absolutely wrong—wrong in all possible circumstances—to break a promise, it is always something which must be done with moral regret. Christian tradition has always interpreted the commandment forbidding killing in the same kind of way. It is intrinsically wrong, because of the kind of action it is; it has not been considered absolutely wrong, for people have believed it permissible in just wars, or in cases of capital punishment. But the repetition of the simple principle that one ought never to kill serves as a reminder of the enormous importance of human life in our morality as a whole.

A final purpose of moral principles is to keep some ideals before us, even if we know that they are forever beyond our reach. Thus we might say that it is our duty as Christians to be perfect, that we should love one another as we love ourselves, or that husbands and wives should have a love which is as deep as Christ's love for his body the Church. It is not that we expect this of ourselves. It is rather that we are using these ideals to try to make sure that we never rest with a comfortable mediocrity.

It is important to be clear about which kind of principle we are using, and what we are using it for. If someone took a principle about the duty to be perfect as if it were a recipe for everyday action, the likely result is that they would develop a debilitating scrupulosity which would have quite the opposite result to what they desired. If someone takes a summary-reminder principle, say about promise-keeping, as saying all that has to be said on the subject, they will make many a moral mistake. But there is one important qualification which is worth making here. There are times when it is very useful to use over-simplified principles as if they did express the whole truth. Obviously this is true in the case of younger children, who would simply be confused by being given the kind of complex principles which an adult might try to live by. But I think the same goes for all of us at times, when, for one reason or another, we are not confident of our adult judgement. Two examples will illustrate what I mean. It might be, for instance, that there are occasions on which it would be of great benefit all round to reveal information which was given to one in confidence—say, in a professional relationship. Yet one might not be at all sure of one's judgement in deciding which cases are which; and rather than adopt a policy of trying to decide each time, one might well believe that it would be better to adopt a policy that such information will *never* be revealed. It may be better to live by a possibly over-simple principle than to risk the dangers of trying to live by one which is more accurate, but more tricky to apply correctly. Again, one might well believe that there are occasions on which to have teachers administer corporal punishment would be the best solution to a problem. One does not, then, believe that to adminster such punishment is always wrong. Nevertheless, one might be sufficiently afraid of the abuses and damage which might occur if teachers had to decide each time whether this was one of the occasions on which it would be right, that one prefers to adopt the simpler view that to adminster corporal punishment is wrong.

Enough has been said, I think, to show that there is a very proper place for moral rules in our moral thinking, but that they play a variety of roles which it is important to keep distinct. It would indeed be a travesty of the Gospel to worship rules for their own sake. But it seems to me equally to be a very naïve view of ourselves to suppose that we have no use for them, once they are properly understood.

A Morality for All Nations

It is part of the glory of God's creative power that human beings are capable of such rich diversity, and can find their fulfilment in so many different ways. Men and women can find fulfilment in marriage, or in an unmarried life. Some need a high degree of education, others do not; some live in a small family circle, others in extended families with a quite different pattern of affections, duties and expectations. Some are artists, some factory workers, some peasants; some are members of a tribe, others of a one-party state, others still are good democrats. There is no one rigid pattern of life to which all must conform in order to find their fulfilment. To be sure, any society, culture or way of life which is going to hold out the genuine possibility of fulfilment for a human being will have to respond somehow or other to all the basic drives which we all share. To that extent, there will be an underlying similarity between any moral codes which succeed in responding to people's needs. But we have already noticed how diverse are the ways in which we can learn to interpret our needs, and how diverse are the choices we can legitimately make between needs which conflict. It follows that the details of the moral codes which different people will observe may legitimately be very different; it is not just that someone who is married, for example, will have duties which an unmarried person does not, true though that is. It may also be that an arranged

57

marriage may violate the rights of the individual within one cultural context, and may not do so at all within another. Different cultures represent extremely complex and subtle balances between the various needs that people have, and needs that are not met in one way will be met in another. For this reason, elements from one culture cannot be simply grafted on to another, without tending to disrupt everything else in the process.

It follows, I believe, that if Christian morality is to be a morality for all nations to whom the Gospel is to be preached, it cannot be expressed just in terms of one particular culture, not even the culture in which the Christian faith first grew and flourished. It should be our joy as Christians to welcome the richness and diversity of other cultures and other moral codes, wherever those cultures lead men and women to their true fulfilment. We should not lightly assume that a culture cannot be truly fulfilling just because it is different from our own, or different from the culture in which the Gospels were written. We should not, therefore, carelessly seek to alter the morality of another culture in the name of Christian morality.

So we may conclude with one final reflection, both sobering and inspiring. We have not yet learnt all that Christ is and means, for we have not yet learnt what it is for the members of his body to be truly Chinese, or Indian or African. We have not yet learnt the full extent of Christian morality until we have learnt all we can from Christians in cultures other than our own, and seen how their moralities can be illuminated by the faith we all share. When we learn that, we may discover more about ourselves in the process, and begin to see why it is that in our Father's house there are many mansions.

FURTHER READING

G. R. Dunstan, (ed.), *Duty and Discernment*. London, S.C.M. Press, 1975

Joseph Fuchs, S.J., *Human Values and Christian Morality*. London, Gill and Macmillan, 1970

James M. Gustafson, *Can Ethics be Christian?* Chicago and London, University of Chicago Press, 1975

————*Protestant and Roman Catholic Ethics:* Prospects for Rapprochement. London, S.C.M. Press, 1978

John Macquarrie, *Three Issues in Ethics*. London, S.C.M. Press, 1970

John Passmore, *The Perfectibility of Man*. London, Duckworth, 1970.

Practical Theology Series
Edited by Edmund Flood and John Coventry